Standing on the Promises

Also by Steve May

It's All in the Dailies
Sheepish: A Study of Psalm 23
Never Lose Heart (2 Corinthians 4:16-18)
Here Comes Trouble (2 Chronicles 20)
Like a Rock (1 Thessalonians)
Preaching Through the Year
Back to Basics Preaching
Walk the Talk (1 Peter)
Sixty Sermons

STANDING ON THE PROMISES

REDISCOVER THE SOLID GROUND
BENEATH YOUR FAITH

STEVE MAY

ALDERSON PRESS
NASHVILLE

Standing on the Promises
© 2026 by Steve May
ISBN: 978-1-964597-02-7

This volume includes original material by Steve May previously published at PreachingLibrary.com

Special thanks to Barry Brown for his invaluable input throughout this process, and to Dot Hatfield for proofing the final manuscript.

All Scripture quotations, unless otherwise indicated, are taken from the Holy Bible, New International Version®, NIV®. Copyright ©1973, 1978, 1984, 2011 by Biblica, Inc.™ Used by permission of Zondervan. All rights reserved worldwide. The "NIV" and "New International Version" are trademarks registered in the United States Patent and Trademark Office by Biblica, Inc.™

Scripture quotations marked (NLT) are taken from the Holy Bible, New Living Translation, copyright ©1996, 2004, 2015 by Tyndale House Foundation. Used by permission of Tyndale House Publishers, Inc., Carol Stream, Illinois 60188. All rights reserved.

Scripture quotations marked (TLB) are taken from The Living Bible, copyright © 1971 by Tyndale House Foundation. Used by permission of Tyndale House Foundation, Carol Stream, Illinois 60188. All rights reserved.

Scripture quotations marked (ESV) are from The ESV® Bible (The Holy Bible, English Standard Version®), copyright © 2001 by Crossway, a publishing ministry of Good News Publishers. Used by permission. All rights reserved.

Scripture quotations marked (NASB) are taken from the New American Standard Bible, Copyright © 1977, 1995 by The Lockman Foundation. Used by permission. All rights reserved.

Scripture quotations marked (Aramaic Bible) are from the Original Aramaic New Testament in Plain English with Psalms & Proverbs Copyright © 2007; 8th edition Copyright © 2013 All rights reserved. Used by Permission.

Scripture marked (NKJV) is taken from the New King James Version®. Copyright © 1982 by Thomas Nelson. Used by permission. All rights reserved.

For more information about our preaching and teaching resources, visit aldersonpress.com

Published by:
Alderson Press
2817 West End Avenue #126-168
Nashville TN 37203

For Gabriel

CONTENTS

FOREWORD 1

1. The Promise of Faithfulness 5

2. The Promise of God's Presence 17

3. The Promise of a Life That Matters 27

4. The Promise of Ultimate Good 39

5. The Promise of Answered Prayer 49

6. The Promise of Perfect Peace 59

7. The Promise of Plenty 69

8. The Promise of God's Cancel-Free Covenant 79

The Next Step 91

FOREWORD

Promises are often easy to make and hard to keep.

We've all had moments when someone gave their word and walked away, never to return. Maybe we've done the same. Life is spiked with broken promises. Over time it can make you wonder: Can anyone be trusted?

This is why the promises of God matter so much.

They're not subject to the whim of the times. Neither are they based on how you feel. They come from the heart of a faithful Father who never goes back on His Word.

This book is a journey through eight of those promises. These have carried me — and a multitude of others — through countless storms. They're an anchor in the midst of life's wind and waves. And they'll remind you again and again that you are not alone.

My prayer is that these words will meet you right where you are and stay with you long after you've turned the final page of this book.

You can build your life on what God has spoken. You can take Him at His Word. When everything else gets shaken, you can stand on His every promise.

Steve May
January 2026

Whereby are given unto us exceeding great and precious promises: that by these ye might be partakers of the divine nature.
2 Peter 1:4

THE PROMISE OF FAITHFULNESS

A Promise Made is a Promise Kept.
Psalm 145

IN THE REAL WORLD, a promise made doesn't always mean a promise kept.

Political campaigns, for example, are built on promises: If elected, I'll do this and I'll do that. And, of course, we've come to expect a certain percentage of these promises—perhaps a huge percentage—to remain unfulfilled. It's just part of the game.

It's the same in business. Whether you're buying a car or booking a flight, the price advertised is often significantly less than the price you pay, thanks to small print and added fees. Consumers don't like it when it happens, but sellers do it just the same.

Worst of all, this habit extends to personal relationships. Friends are friends forever, so they say, but friendships sometimes dissolve. Love, meant to be eternal, has been known to wither. We've come to expect it.

It feels like more promises are broken than kept.

Unfortunately, that's just the way of this wounded world. In contrast, however, there is One whose promises are never forgotten, never broken. Like no other, the God we serve stands by everything He says.

This is good news for you and me because His promises apply to every area of life. And His promises are many. In fact, even more than many. According to *The Dictionary of Bible Themes*, there are 5,467 promises in Scripture. Just imagine: if a book were to cover each promise at the rate of one per page, the published result would be two feet thick.

In this collection of studies, we'll focus on eight fundamental promises—personal and powerful—to examine more closely in the pages to come. These provide a foundation upon which you can build your life.

When you compare the precious promises of God's Word with the harsh realities of daily life, maybe you see an ever-widening gap. You're not the only one. God promises so much, yet we experience so little.

It doesn't have to be that way. You can walk in the blessed fulfillment and joyful expectation of God's goodness every single day. This is the abundant life Jesus spoke about: you see blessings unfolding today while anticipating even more tomorrow.

This begins with accepting the Bible's fundamental claims about these exceeding great and precious promises.

ALL REALLY DOES MEAN ALL

His promises apply to you, just as they apply to everyone. They aren't true in a merely general sense for some; they're true in specific sense for all. Including you. As David declared, "The Lord is faithful to all His promises and loving toward all He has made." (Psalm 145:13)

All God's promises apply to all God's people. No restrictions. This was the message Peter preached in Cornelius' house, as noted in Acts 10:34-35: "God does not show favoritism but accepts from every nation the one who fears Him and does what is right."

God's promises aren't based on race or culture, age or generation. Neither are they based on your own worthiness. They're for everyone, anywhere. *Including you*. Joy, peace, happiness, purpose, fulfillment, provision, abundance, blessing, and protection are yours for the taking, when you're ready to receive them.

In Psalm 145, the word "all" (or its equivalent) appears more than a dozen times. King David intends to convey an all-encompassing message: all of God's promises belong to all of God's people.

One notable distinction between Biblical literature and other historical religious texts—especially those of ancient Greece—is the use of the word "promise." In other cultures, it typically refers to a human commitment made to the gods, but rarely to the gods' commitment to humans. The idea of gods making promises to humans was virtually non-existent.

Yahweh, the God of Israel, is the notable exception. He stands out from the others. He is a "try me, test me, prove me" kind of God. He is an "I will give My Word and I will keep My Word" kind of God.

Each and every promise of Scripture is true. And each and every one is directed, in some way, to you.

With God, a promise made is a promise kept. This is why the Apostle Paul wrote, "For all the promises of God find their Yes in him. That is why it is through him that we utter our Amen to God for his glory." (2 Corinthians 1:20 ESV)

All really means all. Living a promise-filled life begins with saying, "I choose to believe the promises of God, each and every one. I accept them as meant for all His people, including me."

GOD KNOWS THE RIGHT
TIME ALL THE TIME

King David said, "The eyes of all look to You, and You give them their food at the proper time." (Psalm 145:16) Notice the phrase is "at the proper time." Not "the preferred time." This distinction matters because for many of us the preferred time would have been yesterday.

We often pray, "Lord, thank you for this wonderful promise. I will claim it for myself and wait for it in faith. Now, if you don't mind my asking, what's taking so long?" I don't know about you, but that sounds a little like me sometimes.

The key to living in the flow of God's promises is understanding that the promise-filled life involves a two-part process. One part is anticipation, the other is realization. Not every promise will be fulfilled yesterday, or today, or even tomorrow. Sometimes, there is a necessary season of waiting.

So, when is the promise fulfilled?

At the proper time.

A pastor I know had been waiting years to plant a church, facing delay after delay. This went for more than a decade. Then, seemingly from nowhere, an opportunity arose. He and his family moved to a new city to launch an exciting new work.

He later said, "I'm so thankful I didn't do this ten years ago. I wasn't ready for the challenge. I'm glad God waited until the time was right."

Another friend waited into her thirties to get married—and it wasn't her choice. She was eager to meet Mr. Right, but he remained as elusive as ever. And it felt to her like God wasn't helping.

Then, out of the blue, the right man came along. They dated, became engaged, and eventually married. They're now living the happily-ever-after phase of their story.

She later expressed gratitude that they hadn't met in their younger days, as they probably wouldn't have liked like each other all that much. God allowed them to wait until they knew what they were looking for, and were equipped for the challenge of building a life together. While others may be ready to take this step at a younger age, they needed more time. So, at the proper time, God brought them together.

In a promise-filled life, there will be seasons of expectation where the promise remains unfulfilled. During this time, it's easy to become discouraged. It's tempting to throw up your hands and say, "Since it didn't happen yesterday, it feels like it'll never happen at all."

Over the years, I've sometimes found myself saying, "God, you promised an abundant life. Why, then, does my life feel anything but abundant? You promised joy, but I feel only despair. You promised a life of purpose, but it's like I'm sitting on the bench. You promised victory, but these days I'm in constant retreat."

It's a common misconception about God's promises: "If I'm not experiencing it right this moment, the promise must not be real."

Now, most of us wouldn't abandon the faith simply because a promise didn't appear to be fulfilled. But here's what we might do: We might give up hope. We might get cynical about it. We might lower our expectations for the life we want. Instead of using this in-between season to grow in our faith and find joy in the Lord, we just might resign ourselves to complaining.

I have firsthand experience here. There have been many times when God has come through for our ministry, ultimately providing what He promised from the very beginning. I later realized that instead of enduring the season-of-waiting with an attitude of joyful expectation, I squandered it with complaints—simply because I wanted the promise fulfilled at my preferred time rather than God's proper time.

God will come through when the time is right. Living your life in the flow of His promises means you're ready to embrace both the days of anticipation and the days of realization.

IT'S MOSTLY ABOUT LIVING IN JOYFUL EXPECTATION

You can wait each day in joyful expectation because you know fulfillment is on its way, even if you don't yet see it. The promises of God are "yes" and "amen," and you have the courage to build your life on that belief. So when something doesn't happen as quickly as you'd like, you can say, "No problem, no panic. It'll happen at God's appointed time." You can say, as the prophet said, "But as for me, I watch in hope for the Lord; I wait for God my Savior. My God will hear me." (Micah 7:7)

The secret to getting started in joyful expectation is found in a single word tucked away in this ancient hymn of praise:

"They shall abundantly utter the memory of Thy great goodness, and shall sing of Thy righteousness." (Psalm 145:7 KJV)

The key word? *Memory*.

In this psalm, as in many others, David emphasizes the importance of remembering the great and mighty works God has performed for His people throughout history.

What if you made it a point to remember how God has come through for you—and those close to you—again and again? What if you kept a list of every prayer answered and every promise fulfilled? You could refer to this list during the in-between seasons while you're waiting for the next to come your way.

Remembering God's past goodness not only helps you maintain a grateful attitude, it also strengthens your oft-waning faith. It keeps at bay that bothersome sense of entitlement. It reminds us, yet again, that we have no reason to be impatient.

When we remember what God has done in the past, it's easier to face the season of in-between with joyful expectation, because we know that God can, and will, do it again.

It makes sense, then, to say that the secret to living a promise-filled life is a good memory.

CLOSING THOUGHTS

Imagine that a top executive from one of the world's leading companies reaches out to you with an offer too good to refuse: a dream job with an incredible salary bound with an unbreakable guarantee. And then he says, "By the way, we want you to start in six months."

What would you do? Well, of course, you'd accept the job. And then what? Wait six months to throw a party? I don't think so. You'd begin the celebration immediately, even while you wait.

It's the same with living a promise-filled life. You can approach each day of joyful expectation with an attitude of celebration, knowing that God's promises are "yes" and "amen." And He will make it happen at exactly the right time.

How can you be sure?

You *remember*. You remind yourself daily of all the good things God has done for His people, including you.

You can celebrate today in joyful expectation of the goodness coming your way.

Why?

Because with our great God, a promise made is a promise kept.

BUILDING MOMENTUM: LIVING A PROMISE EMPOWERED LIFE

1 Are there promises you struggle to believe, thinking they're mean for everyone but you? Try inserting your name into the promise:

"If Robert confesses his sins, God is faithful and just to forgive..." (1 John 1:9)

"I have come that Carl might have life, and have it more abundantly..." (John 10:10)

"I will never leave you, Brenda, or forsake you..." (Hebrews 13:8)

How does it feel to hear your name spoken in words of Scripture?

_____

_____

_____

2 Are there promises you're waiting to see fulfilled in your life? Consider making a list. And then, as Isaiah 43:26 says, "bring them to God's remembrance" in prayer.

3 Have you ever given up on a promise too soon? What made you let go? What would it take to claim this promise again?

4 Can you remember a promise that was fulfilled later than expected, but turned out to be right on time?

5 God has promised to answer prayer, to work all things together for good, to meet our needs. Which of these have you seen fulfilled in your life? Share a moment when God surprised you with His timing, provision, or grace.

NOTES & IDEAS

NOTES & IDEAS

THE PROMISE OF GOD'S PRESENCE

He is With You Every Step of the Way.
Judges 6:12

LET'S FOLLOW UP on a verse from our previous study. "The Lord is near to all who call upon Him, to all who call upon Him in truth." (Psalm 145:18 NKJV) What does this mean? And how can it influence our daily decisions?

Most of us readily affirm that God is "everywhere" in a vague and general way. But we sometimes doubt that God is genuinely here, with us, in this very moment, wherever we may be. At times, it seems we believe God is everywhere *but here*. When we don't feel His presence, it leads us to neglect His presence. And when we neglect His presence, we miss out on experiencing His promises.

Here's a story from the early days of Gideon's life. He would later become Judge over Israel. He's considered now to be one of the greatest of the era. This was unexpected back then, because in his younger years he appeared to lack the self-confidence necessary to lead.

What made the difference for Gideon?

The presence of God.

During this time in Israel's history there was no king or centralized government. Israel existed as a confederacy of 12 independent tribes led by a series of judges, united only by their faith in the God of Abraham—the one who revealed Himself to Moses as the great I AM.

For several years, various nomadic tribes, including a group known as the Midianites, had been invading Israel and depleting their resources. Some Israelites were forced to seek refuge in caves just to thresh their grain in secret. This is what Gideon was doing when an angel appeared to him, saying, "The Lord is with you, mighty warrior." (Judges 6:12)

The angel then told Gideon that he would be the one to lead Israel to victory against the Midianites. Although Gideon had his doubts, he did become a crucial figure in saving Israel—not only from their enemies, but from themselves as well.

In previous years, the Israelites had done evil in the sight of the Lord. Under Gideon's leadership, they entered a new season of obedience, all beginning with the angel of the Lord assuring this timid young man: "The Lord is with you."

What was true in Gideon's case is also true for you. The Lord is with you. He's not just everywhere. He's *here*—wherever you are.

In Matthew 28:20, Jesus' final words to His followers were, "I am with you every day, even unto the end of time." (Matthew 28:20, Aramaic Bible) Additionally, in the book of Hebrews, He makes this promise: "Never will I leave you; never will I forsake you." (Hebrews 13:5)

You can experience the truth of these words every day. It's not always something you'll see or feel, but it *is* something you can know: God is with me.

Experiencing His presence everyday comes down to acknowledging His presence everyday, regardless of your circumstances or emotions. It's a habit you can cultivate.

SOMETIMES YOU WONDER WHY, AND THAT'S OK

The angel approached Gideon and said, "The Lord is with you." Gideon responded by asking, in effect, "If the Lord is with us, then why are things the way they are? Why are we suffering? Where are the miracles we've heard about from long ago?" He then said that it seemed, from his perspective, that God had abandoned them.

At times, we find ourselves asking similar questions, both on a cultural and personal level. If God is with us, why is everything such a mess?

The angel didn't scold Gideon for his candor, but neither did he offer a direct answer. Instead of focusing on the why, he provided Gideon with a "what's next." He said, in effect, "Never mind *why*. You're about to deliver Israel from the hand of Midian."

It's OK to ask "why." Just know that the response you receive will often be in the form of "what's next." You can pray, "Lord, why don't you do something about this?" Just be ready for Him to say, "I was about to ask you the same thing."

When you ask "why," God's response is often an invitation to do something about it.

SOMETIMES YOU QUESTION YOUR QUALIFICATIONS

After Gideon asked why things were the way they were, the Bible says that the Lord turned to him and said, "Go in the strength you have and save Israel out of Midian's hand." (Judges 6:14)

Gideon responded, in effect, "How could it be me? My family is the least in my tribe, and I am the least in my family." The Lord answered Gideon, saying, "I will be with you, and you will strike down all the Midianites, leaving none alive." (Judges 6:16)

Gideon was right where God wanted him to be. It's where God wants you to be as well—where you're not relying on your own credentials or personal skills to fulfill His calling.

God calls us beyond our abilities. He asks us to do more than we could ever do on our own, so that we have no choice but to rely on His strength. He is a God who says, "Not by might nor by power, but by My Spirit." (Zechariah 4:6)

Even Moses felt that God's calling on his life was beyond his reach. He couldn't imagine being the one to lead God's chosen people out of Egypt. He knew himself too well. So, he asked God, "Who am I that I should be able to accomplish such a thing?" God responded to Moses, just as he did with Gideon: "I will be with you." (Exodus 3:12)

The same is true for you. Wherever God calls you, wherever He leads you, He will be with you. His presence will be the difference in what your life becomes.

It's OK to question your qualifications, because every time you do, you're reminding yourself that in your own strength, you cannot fulfill God's calling on your life. You need the power of His presence.

SOMETIMES YOU NEED CONFIRMATION

After Gideon was told about his mission, he said, in effect, "If this is true, prove it. Give me a sign." He then took some rather elaborate steps, leaving the angel waiting while going home to roast a goat and bake some bread. Upon his return, the angel indeed gave Gideon a sign to confirm that everything was true: he touched the food, and it was consumed by fire, going up in smoke. At that point, Gideon knew the message was genuine.

Later on, Gideon sought further confirmation. He placed a fleece (a wool covering) on the ground and prayed, "If you will use me to deliver Israel from the Midianites, let this fleece be wet with dew tomorrow morning while the rest of the ground remains dry." (Judges 12:36–37)

When he awoke the next morning, the ground was dry, and the fleece was wet. To ensure it wasn't a coincidence, Gideon prayed once more, asking for the opposite result. The following morning, he found the ground wet and the fleece dry.

The practice of laying out a fleece before the Lord is significant. A crucial distinction is that Gideon did not ask God to reveal His will out of nowhere; he sought confirmation of a word God had already spoken.

Sometimes, when we're about to take a step of faith, we do need some kind of assurance. It's essential to be certain that we have genuinely heard God's voice and clearly understand the path He is calling us to take.

In seeking confirmation, today we have resources that Gideon did not. We have the Word of God, the Bible, which can confirm His will for our lives. Additionally, we have spiritual leaders to whom we can turn for wisdom and counsel.

If you're unsure of your next step, you can ask for a little more direction. Sometimes, God will take control of an outcome to provide you with clear guidance. More often, though, He offers confirmation through His Word and through the godly people He has placed around you.

It's perfectly acceptable to ask God to confirm His will. You can say with confidence: "God, as I seek to walk in faith, I want to be sure that it's Your voice I'm hearing, not just my imagination. Please provide me with the direction I need."

CLOSING THOUGHTS

The idea that it's OK to ask why, to question your qualifications, and to confirm your understanding of God's will is rooted in the belief that God is not distant. He is here. He is with you. He walks with you and talks with you, and He tells you that you're His own.

Let's revisit the first words spoken by the angel to Gideon:

"The Lord is with you, mighty warrior."

What did he call Gideon? "Mighty Warrior."

Here he was: an apprehensive young man, the least of the least, hiding out in a cave, in fear of the enemy. And he was called Mighty Warrior.

God was speaking to Gideon's future, not his past, or even his present. He addressed the man Gideon was destined to become. Just as Jesus called Simon "the Rock" long before he lived up to that name, God called Gideon Mighty Warrior before he ever drew his sword.

How was Gideon able to be called Mighty Warrior?

He had one qualifying attribute: The Lord was with him.

Here's the lesson to learn. God's presence in your life brings out your best. He empowers you to do what needs to be done. He enables you to rise above your limitations. And, in moments of doubt, He gives you the assurance you need.

Now, here's something to do sometime when you're out there in the real world. Look at where you're standing and take note of all that's going on around you. Then remind yourself: "He is here. Right here, right now. And His presence in this moment is sure to bring out the very best in me."

BUILDING MOMENTUM: LIVING EACH DAY IN THE PRESENCE OF GOD

1 Most of us have asked, at some point, "Why this? Why me? Why now?" But what if the more important question is, "What's next?" Could it be that God is calling you forward into something new? What might that next step look like?

2 Have you ever faced an opportunity that felt beyond your qualifications? Is it wrong to say yes to something that seems bigger than you? Share a time when God gave you strength to do something you couldn't have done on your own.

3 Have you ever placed a fleece before God, asking for a clear sign? What was the situation? And how did His response (or His silence) guide your next step?

___

___

___

4 Scripture is one of the clearest ways God speaks to us. Has there been a moment when a Biblical text gave you direction or clarity about his calling on your life?

___

___

___

5 Who are the godly voices God has placed around you? In which ways have you leaned on their wisdom to confirm His voice?

___

___

___

6 When you don't feel God's presence, how do you remind yourself that He is still with you? Have you ever come through a season of doubt to realize He was closer than you thought?

___

___

___

NOTES & IDEAS

THE PROMISE OF
A LIFE THAT MATTERS

We Find Our Purpose in Serving Others.
Ephesians 2:8-10

A FEW YEARS AGO, while my mom was away at a writer's retreat, I watched over her house, bringing in the mail, watering the plants, and emptying the fridge.

She lives on the main street of a small town in Arkansas. One morning, I noticed a crowd gathering in the front yard, with folks setting up lawn chairs and making themselves comfortable. I sent her a message, and she quickly replied, "I forgot to tell you. Today is the big parade. It begins at 10. You should watch it if you can."

I had some business to attend to in a nearby town. I tried to get back early because, I mean, who doesn't love a parade? You've got marching bands, decorated floats, and local celebrities in convertible cars tossing candy in your direction. It's hard to resist.

Unfortunately, I got back a little late. By the time I pulled into the driveway, the streets were empty. The lawn chairs were gone. There was nothing left to see except the inevitable litter a crowd leaves behind. Even that wouldn't last long; the street cleaners were already making their rounds.

There was a parade right there in the front yard, and I missed it.

And now, I'll let you in on a secret: this isn't the only time I've felt like I missed the parade. Maybe you know that feeling, too.

Sometimes we wonder: Are the best things gone for good? Am I doing what I should be doing, or is life just passing me by?

The promise in this study may not be the most obvious promise of all, but it's certainly among the most precious. It concerns the meaning of life and what we should be doing about it. And it relates to this parade that we're all part of.

Here's the promise: You have a purpose. There's a reason you're here. Best of all, you can discover this reason and put it into practice every day of your life. There's no risk of the parade passing you by, because you're in the parade. You have a role to play in the production.

THE CAST OF CHARACTERS

Consider the many participants of such an event.

You have the spectators lined up along the streets, eager to be entertained.

Then there are the judges perched high at Parade Central. Their job is to evaluate the worthiness of every float and the merits of every demonstration.

Next, you have those in the spotlight—the ones who march in step, carry banners, ride scooters, wear funny hats, and throw candy to the crowd.

And then there are those behind the scenes. The production crew. They spend weeks preparing every detail, decorating their floats, securing permits, and, of course, purchasing large bags of sweets.

The production crew also includes someone that no one sees, someone who's there long after everyone else has gone home.

You'll find that person cleaning up debris and putting everything back where it belongs.

The true heroes of the parade are never at risk of missing out because they're the ones who make it happen.

The same can be said for you. Yes, there's a parade, and it's not passing you by. You're in it. You're not just a spectator, and you're not merely a judge; you're one of the ones getting it done. Sometimes your role is to ride in the limo and wave; other times, it's to sweep up after everyone goes home.

If you've ever felt like you're missing out on life, it could be that you want to experience it as a spectator, or to observe it all from the judge's platform. But God calls you to full participation.

You have a purpose. You have a reason for being here. And a major role to play. One part of life's adventure is discovering your role. The other part is putting it into practice.

While the specifics of your calling will differ from everyone else's, there is a general characteristic of God's calling that applies to us all. Paul talked about it when he said, "For we are God's handiwork, created in Christ Jesus to do good works, which God prepared in advance for us to do." (Ephesians 2:10)

The context here is significant. Paul had just finished saying that we are saved by grace through faith, not by works, so that no one can boast. We're not saved by good works, but we're created for the purpose of doing good works. Peter once summed up Jesus' life by saying, "He went around doing good." (Acts 10:38) This should summarize our lives as well.

These good works that we've been created to do are not intended to get us into heaven. They're intended to get us through life.

Doing good work makes living worthwhile. Just like being part of the parade beats merely watching it, any day of the week.

We're called to a life of good works, which means we're called to a life of service. This means we go around doing good. Let's consider what that looks like.

A LIFE OF SERVICE BRINGS BENEFIT TO OTHERS

Jesus said, "Whoever wants to become great among you must be your servant..." He emphasized that even he, the king of kings, came not to be served but to serve. [cf. Matt. 20:26-28] Regardless of your specific calling—whether it relates to your career, location, or family situation—you can be sure that it will involve serving others.

Consider how virtually every job centers, in some way, around service. And consider how we sometimes approach our jobs with a non-servant's heart. We find ourselves asking, "How can I do this in a way that requires the least amount of effort?" This attitude undermines our success in the workplace and in life.

Viktor Frankl was an Austrian physician who spent years in a Nazi death camp during World War II. In his book, *Man's Search for Meaning*, he tells how those who maintained their strength and sanity amid such suffering were the ones who sought to serve the other prisoners, and who shared what little they had with one another. Their ability to cope was bolstered by their kindness, their compassion, and their willingness to focus on something beyond themselves.

While our experiences do not compare to the inhumanity they faced, we can still follow their example by concentrating on the good we do for others. Solomon said, "Whoever refreshes others will be refreshed." (Proverbs 11:25)

Legendary basketball coach John Wooden once said, "You cannot live a perfect day without doing something for someone who will never be able to repay you."

So, each day we can ask ourselves: How will I bring benefit to the lives of those around me?

A LIFE OF SERVICE DIRECTS ATTENTION TO GOD

In the 1990s, a high-profile billionaire made headlines announcing his pledge to donate one billion dollars to charity — quite an impressive sum at that time. While this gift is certainly noteworthy, it's also true that, due to tax benefits and an extended distribution schedule, the donation didn't significantly impact his net worth. However, it did earn him a spot on the cover of Newsweek, which naturally boosted his celebrity status.

My point is not to criticize this billionaire, especially since his charitable contributions exceed mine by almost a billion dollars. My point is that we should be cautious of any PR aspect of our giving. Jesus taught that when we do good for others, our left hand shouldn't know what our right hand is doing. [cf. Matthew 6:3] The goal should be to glorify God, not ourselves.

The Apostle Peter affirms this idea: "Each of you should use whatever gift you have received to serve others...so that in all things God may be praised through Jesus Christ." (1 Peter 4:10-12) This is the fundamental difference in living a life of service. We don't perform good works for our own benefit. In fact, we're not even looking for acknowledgment. We act to glorify God, as expressed by the psalmist, "Not to us, LORD, not to us, but to Your name be the glory." (Psalm 115:1)

I once heard a man who had spent years living homeless share that sometimes people would give him money while saying, "I do this in the name of the Lord Jesus Christ." This simple phrase helped him realize that he was more than just an object of pity; he was someone whom Jesus cares about. It sparked his curiosity to learn more.

A question worth asking: Will my actions today draw attention to me or to God?

A LIFE OF SERVICE BRINGS YOU CLOSER TO GOD

If someone were to ask, "How can I get closer to God?" the answer might include suggestions such as devoting yourself to prayer, immersing yourself in the Word, singing hymns, attending church, reading Christian books, and listening to preaching podcasts. These are all commendable steps in the right direction, and I would certainly recommend them.

However, if you want to fast-track your journey to a closer walk with God, I suggest you serve. Do something for someone that they cannot do for themselves. And if possible, do it under the radar. No one else needs to know about it.

The Son of Man came not to be served, but to serve. When you serve, you become more like Him. When you go around doing good, you imitate Jesus.

CLOSING THOUGHTS

Back to parades. When Winston Churchill addressed a group of labor leaders in the early days of World War II, he asked them to imagine a grand victory procession on the streets of London, where all the heroes of the war would be celebrated: the foot soldiers fighting in the trenches, the dedicated sailors protecting the borders, and the courageous aviators executing attacks behind enemy lines.

Coming next, Churchill said, would be a long line of sweat-stained, soot-streaked men in miner's caps. He said someone might ask, "Where were you during the critical days of conflict?" And from ten thousand voices would come the answer: "We were deep in the earth with our faces to the coal!"

Not all service is visible to the crowd. Those on the royal floats are quite prominent, but the ones who sweep often go unnoticed. Both are essential to the parade's success.

Your service to God is essential, as well. Sometimes you'll receive grand recognition. Other times you'll feel like the kingdom's best-kept secret.

Rest assured, your Father sees everything you do and He's pleased with your good works. Through your efforts, you fulfill the purpose for which you were created: You build up others, you bring glory to His name, and you become more like Jesus.

Your good works won't earn you a place in heaven, but they were never intended to. They will, however, help you navigate this life on earth. With each act of service, you make good on the reason you're here.

BUILDING MOMENTUM: PUTTING YOUR PURPOSE INTO PRACTICE

1 What are some things that make us feel like we're missing out on life? Which false definitions of "meaning" do we sometimes chase?

_____

_____

_____

_____

2 Are you ever tempted to judge the parade rather than join in? What does full participation in life look like for you right now?

_____

_____

_____

_____

3 How does your current job—or the work you do each day—benefit others? What would it look like to become more intentionally focused on serving others through your work?

_____

_____

_____

_____

4 Can you think of a time when you did something kind or meaningful that no one else noticed? How did it feel to not be recognized? What kept you going?

_____

_____

_____

5 In which ways are you being called to increase your service to others? Where might God be nudging you to invest your time or energy next?

_____

_____

_____

6 Are you willing to serve even when no one knows about it? Why is it so hard to do this? How can we teach ourselves to grow in this area?

_____

_____

_____

_____

NOTES & IDEAS

NOTES & IDEAS

THE PROMISE OF ULTIMATE GOOD

This Situation is Certainly Better Than it Seems.
Romans 8:28

LET'S BEGIN WITH the story of Joseph, the beloved son of Jacob. He was the one, you may remember, with the Amazing Technicolor Dreamcoat.

Joseph's status as his father's favorite made him the least favorite among his eleven brothers. One day, while working in the fields, they hatched a devious plot: they sold him into slavery and told their father he'd been killed by a wild animal. Jacob was devastated.

Joseph was taken to Egypt and sold into the household of Potiphar, a government official. He worked diligently, earning Potiphar's favor. And then Potiphar's wife falsely accused him of misconduct after he rejected her advances. As a result, Joseph was thrown into prison.

While there, he interpreted a dream for a fellow inmate connected to Pharaoh. Years later, when Pharaoh had troubling dreams of his own, the man (now released) remembered Joseph's unique gift. He was then summoned right away, and he explained to Pharaoh the dream's meaning. He told him that Egypt would experience seven years of prosperity followed by seven years of famine, so the nation should prepare accordingly.

Pharaoh, quite impressed, put Joseph in charge of the project. Under his leadership, Egypt was ready when famine struck.

Back in Canaan, Jacob and Joseph's brothers were also affected by the global shortage. At the point of starvation, they came to Egypt in search of food, unaware they were asking help from the brother they'd betrayed. After a little back and forth, Joseph eventually revealed his identity. He then forgave them for their mistreatment, and brought the whole family to live in Egypt.

Years later, after Jacob's death, the brothers feared Joseph would take revenge. Joseph assured them it wouldn't happen, saying, "You intended to harm me, but God intended it for good to accomplish what is now being done, the saving of many lives." (Genesis 50:20)

Joseph's story reminds us that God can redeem even the worst circumstances. For those who trust him, everything works together for good—every time.

Maybe you feel you have good reason to doubt this promise. Maybe things happening right now don't much make sense at all. Maybe you've asked, "Why, God, why?"

Sometimes, like Joseph, we eventually see how the pieces fit together. We're able to recognize the good that came from the chaos. Other times, however, the resolution isn't quite so obvious. Still, you can be sure of this: If you let Him, God will take whatever happens in your life and work it for good.

Like all of His promises, this one begins with a step of faith. This means choosing to trust Him even when nothing around you adds up. Call it hope or call it optimism, it's the decision to lean into God's goodness despite your circumstances.

Dietrich Bonhoeffer described this kind of hope when he said:

"The essence of optimism is that it takes no account of the present, but it is a source of inspiration, of vitality and hope where others have

resigned; it enables a man to hold his head high, to claim the future for himself and not to abandon it to his enemy." (Letters and Papers from Prison)

That's how we live: not by dwelling on the way things seem, but by holding tight to the promise that, in time, God will make sense of it all.

In the movie *As Good As It Gets*, Jack Nicholson plays a man consumed by turmoil. As he leaves his psychiatrist's office, passing through a waiting room filled with others struggling through life, he stops and asks, "What if this is as good as it gets?"

For many, that's the fear they face. Life will never get better. The pain of the present will never pass. But that's not what Scripture teaches. In fact, the promise of God is quite the opposite.

This isn't as good as it gets. The best is yet to come. Even when life is difficult, even when hope feels out of reach, you can hold on to this truth: The situation is certainly better than it seems. Why? Because today is temporary, and God's goodness is eternal.

Paul wrote, "And we know that for those who love God all things work together for good, for those who are called according to his purpose. For those whom he foreknew he also predestined to be conformed to the image of his Son." (Romans 8:28–29 ESV) Let's think about what this promise means.

THIS PROMISE BELONGS TO EVERYONE WHO'LL ACCEPT IT

Paul is clear about it. This is for those who love God and are called according to His purpose. But this condition need not exclude anyone. Whoever wants to be included in the promise can be included. What's the qualifier? *Your heart.*

There's a common saying: Everything happens for a reason. But this doesn't mean everything turns out dandy for everyone. If you're living in rebellion, making self-destructive decisions one after another, things won't magically work out for the best. That's not how this promise works.

In fact, without God, the answer to Jack Nicholson's question truly is, "Yes, this is probably as good as it gets."

This promise of Romans 8:28 is for those who have surrendered their lives to Jesus Christ. When you've done this, He begins putting the pieces into place, turning even your worst moments into something new.

What about those who've wandered off the path? Or never bothered to take the path? Maybe that's you, and maybe you've made a mess of things. Maybe you think God is done with you. He's not. When you turn to Him, He welcomes you without hesitation. And then He begins His work of restoration.

No matter where you've been, this promise becomes yours the moment you say "Yes" to His will.

GOD ISN'T BEHIND THE CHAOS

Let's be clear: not everything that happens is good. We live in a fallen world. Bad things happen. Some of them are heartbreaking. And evil. But God can redeem even the worst situations you face.

Some assume that everything that happens must somehow be God's will. It's not.

For example, it's never God's will for someone to sin. Or for one person to harm another. Abuse, injustice, and cruelty are never part of His plan. People suffer because of the choices of others, not the intentions of God. Even so, God can take these very circumstances and bring good from them.

Joseph's life shows this. God didn't coax his brothers to betray him, or lead Potiphar's wife to lie. But He used it all to save many lives.

The same with Paul. It wasn't God who put him in prison. That was the work of the Roman authorities. Yet God used Paul's confinement to produce letters that still guide the church today.

God isn't behind the negative events that occur in your life, but he can use them in such a way that good will come. Even if you can't see it yet, trust that it's coming. You don't have to pretend the pain is pleasant. It hurts, and you can admit it. You can also say: "This isn't good at all—but I know that God will somehow bring good from it."

YOU'RE ON YOUR WAY TO BECOMING MORE LIKE JESUS

Romans 8:29 tells us that God's ultimate purpose is to conform us to the image of His Son. That's what "good" looks like in God's plan: Becoming more like Jesus.

This means that even in suffering, God is shaping you into something eternal. You may not see the reason for your pain, but you can trust that God is using it to refine your heart, your character, and your calling.

And when you become more like Jesus, everyone around you benefits. You have more of His presence and power. Your family, coworkers, and friends are blessed by who you're becoming.

Being like Jesus leads to peace, joy, and a life overflowing with blessing. That's the kind of "good" God is working toward.

This is God's single-minded goal for your life. He uses everything—joy and sorrow, success and failure—to make it happen. And when you're surrendered to him, nothing is wasted.

CLOSING THOUGHTS

I often re-watch past football games from my favorite teams. Even ones from years ago. I'm talking about when they win, of course. Why do I do this? Because I know the outcome. The dropped passes and fumbles don't rattle me like they did on game day. I take every miscue in stride because now I know how it all ends.

Romans 8:28 gives this same kind of confidence in life. No matter what you face—loss, hardship, injustice, confusion—you can trust that God is at work, which means the final outcome will be good. He'll use everything you endure to mold you into the image of His Son.

That's the ultimate good. And when you become like Jesus, it blesses everyone around you.

So hold your head high. Don't give in to despair. Even when life makes no sense, God is writing a story that ends in redemption.

Watch what He can do. See the good that's coming your way.

BUILDING MOMENTUM: EACH DAY SECURED IN GOD'S CARE.

1 Self-check: Are you fully surrendered to the Lordship and leadership of Jesus Christ? Have you positioned yourself spiritually in a way that allows God to work all things together for good? Are there steps you need to take toward deeper surrender?

2 Have you ever blamed a negative event—or even a personal mistake—on God's will? What about self-destructive choices? How can we learn to take responsibility without losing sight of grace? Can you see how repentance doesn't change the past, but it can reshape the future?

3 Can you remember a time when something painful or disappointing eventually led to unexpected good? How did your perspective change during this course of events?

4 Have you ever experienced a setback or a hardship that God was able to use to develop your character or deepen your walk with Him? Can you identify ways in which that experience helped you become more like Christ, as described in Romans 8:29?

_____

_____

_____

5 Romans 8:28 reminds us that God works in all things. Is there a current situation in your life where you're still waiting to see the good? What are some steps you could take to demonstrate your trust in Him — even before you see the outcome?

_____

_____

_____

_____

_____

_____

_____

_____

_____

NOTES & IDEAS

THE PROMISE OF ANSWERED PRAYER

You Can Ask God for Anything.
He Always Knows the Right Answer.
John 15:7

PRAYER COULD BE CALLED Christian Living 101. It's like the introductory course to following Jesus. The Bible has so much to say about it. There are more than 365 references to prayer in Scripture. The countless books written have barely scratched the surface of this powerful privilege granted to us by our loving Heavenly Father.

Which means I have my work cut out for me. There's so much to say, and only so much space. Besides, what hasn't been said? In writing about prayer, I'm aware that I might not be telling you anything new. We already know the basics. My goal, then, is to help us all move prayer from the *Things I Know* column to *Things I Actually Do Every Day*.

The next few pages will focus on one aspect: Answered Prayer. Scripture doesn't just invite us to pray. It assures us that God will answer. This promise changes everything. It lifts prayer beyond the realm of mere meditation. It's more than just a way to commune with God, though that in itself is beyond awesome. Prayer is also how we see God make things happen in our lives. That the King of all Creation would listen and respond to folks like you and me is almost beyond belief.

And yet, it's true. Which makes it all the more troubling when many believers—myself included—treat prayer as a last resort. In fact, I sometimes wonder if skeptics grasp the implications of answered prayer more clearly than we do. They mock the idea because to them it seems absurd, too good to be true. And yet we, who supposedly believe in its power, often treat it like an afterthought.

So what does the Bible say about answered prayer? There are many places to look. Consider these words from Isaiah and Jesus.

"I will answer them before they even call to me. While they are still talking about their needs, I will go ahead and answer their prayers!" (Isaiah 65:24 TLB)

"...for your Father knows exactly what you need even before you ask him." (Matthew 6:8)

"If you abide in Me, and My words abide in you, you will ask what you desire, and it shall be done for you." (John 15:7 NKJV)

These verses reveal that answered prayer involves both a promise and a condition. Let's explore what this means, what it doesn't mean, and why it matters.

ANSWERED PRAYER IS NOT CATCH 22

Many misunderstand what answered prayer really means. Much of the confusion stems from how we interpret the words of Scripture. We tend to think in all-or-nothing terms. If our prayers aren't answered exactly as we hoped, our inner skeptic says, "See? Told you! Prayer doesn't work."

Take John 15:7, for example. "Ask what you desire, and it shall be done for you." We often focus on the second part of the verse while ignoring the first: "If you abide in Me, and My words abide in you..." The promise is real, but it's conditional.

We do the same with Matthew 21:22. "If you believe, you will receive whatever you ask for in prayer." Again, we emphasize the result but overlook the condition: Faith.

To fully understand these verses, we need to consider both parts—the promise and the premise. They work together.

There's another mistaken assumption on our part: Prayer is pointless if it isn't God's will, and unnecessary if it is God's will. Won't God do what He wants to do, with or without our input? Actually, Scripture frames it differently. It's true that God will never grant a request that contradicts His will. But, as mentioned before, not everything that happens is His will.

For example, Scripture tells us that God is "not willing that any should perish, but that all should come to repentance." (2 Peter 3:9) Yet millions die without turning to him. This is not His will. Neither is sin. Or suffering. Still, they exist. Every day, events occur on this wretched planet that are outside His desire for all creation.

This is why Jesus teaches us to pray, "Thy will be done on earth as it is in heaven." (Matthew 6:10) His will is not always done. And prayer is a part of how we bring His will to bear on the world around us.

When we abide in Him, praying in faith as we align our requests with His Word, we position ourselves to see His will unfold around us. But if we believe the myth that answered prayer is some kind of divine catch-22, we'll hesitate even to ask. We'll treat God's promises like fine print in a contract: difficult to decipher, laden with loopholes.

God's promise of answered prayers is not fool's gold. There's no trick behind it. It's a genuine invitation to know Him and to experience the power of His presence.

PRAYER SOMETIMES FEELS LIKE IT COULD BE HIT-OR-MISS

Answered prayer is a mystery. The more you pray, the more you are aware of this. Sometimes the answer is yes. Sometimes it's no. And we can't always predict which will it be.

We pray for healing. Sometimes it comes. Sometimes it doesn't. One person prays for marriage and finds their soulmate. Another prays the same and remains single. When we pray for a job, a raise, or financial help, some prayers are answered right away. Others, not at all.

To the cynic, it all seems so random, like rolling the dice. But spiritual maturity reminds us that God sees more than we see. And He acts from a different perspective.

It's like the world of a toddler trying to make sense of grown-up decisions. One moment they're told to go to bed while it's still light outside. The next, they're woken from a deep sleep. One day they get a cookie for no reason. The next, they're expected to eat broccoli. They may wonder, "Can't you at least be consistent?"

We're not toddlers, but spiritually speaking, we often understand just as little. As Paul wrote, "We see through a glass darkly." (1 Corinthians 13:12) Every now and then we catch a glimpse of eternal truth, but most of the time, we simply don't know why things happen the way they do.

And that's okay.

Don't let what you don't understand prevent you from asking God for what you need. Even when you can't explain all the hows and whys of prayer, you can still experience its power.

When you pray, you do so knowing that God answers according to His wisdom, not your own. He sees the full picture and He always acts in love.

GOD PROVIDES THE RIGHT ANSWER AT THE RIGHT TIME

Has someone ever come to you asking for one kind of help, and you realized they were in need of a different solution altogether?

It's happened to me more than once. Like when I told the mechanic my car needed a new starter. After looking at it, he said, "A new starter won't do any good. What you need is an ignition switch." He could have given me what I asked for, but then, I would have wasted money and my car would still be somewhere on the side of the road. Instead, he gave me what I needed.

God responds in a similar way. We often pray based on what we think is wrong or what we assume we need. But He always knows better. He hears our requests and lovingly says, "You asked for A. But what you need is B. So, here's B."

It's like He hears our prayers and makes them better. Paul says as much in Romans 8:26. "We do not know what we ought to pray for, but the Spirit himself intercedes for us." God translates our prayers. He auto-corrects them, so to speak, aligning them with His will.

This is the miracle of answered prayer. It's not that we always get exactly what we asked for, but that we're given instead what we truly need.

Sometimes, the answer matches our request exactly. Other times, God says, "I have something better in mind."

It's comforting to know that God will never give us the wrong thing just because we asked for it. He invites us to ask freely, and He promises to respond faithfully. Even when we don't know what to say, He hears the cry of our hearts and gives us what we need, according to His perfect will.

CLOSING THOUGHTS

Answered prayer will always retain a measure of mystery. Some of the deepest matters remain elusive. We're like toddlers piecing together a world we don't fully understand, often wondering why we're given broccoli instead of cake.

A good parent welcomes their child's requests, but still makes decisions based on what is truly best. Often, the parent already knows what the child needs and has planned accordingly.

That's who God is. Our loving Father knows exactly what we need, even before we ask.

That's the promise of answered prayer. When you walk with Him—abiding in His Word and allowing His presence to shape your desires—you gain this blessed assurance: You can ask for anything, knowing He will either give you what you ask, or something better.

BUILDING MOMENTUM: FINDING LIFE'S ANSWERS IN ANSWERED PRAYER.

1 What does it really mean to abide in Jesus? How is an abiding life lived out in everyday terms—on a typical morning, or an especially stressful afternoon? Which small habits could help you remain more aware of His presence throughout the day?

2 Can you think of a prayer that didn't get answered, or didn't get answered the way you hoped? Looking back, has your perspective about it changed? What did you learn?

3 Just like toddlers see the world differently as they grow, our view of faith often matures over time. What's changed for you in the past five or ten years? Do you see God—or the world—more clearly now? Less cynically? More hopefully?

4 When you pray, do you tend to focus more on outcomes or connection? What might shift in your prayer life if you focused less on results and more on remaining close to Jesus, even when answers are slow or unclear?

___

___

___

5 Can you think of a time when you prayed for something that you now realize wouldn't have been good for you? Did God answer your prayer in a different way?

___

___

___

___

___

___

___

___

NOTES & IDEAS

THE PROMISE OF PERFECT PEACE

*Keep Your Thoughts Where
They'll Do You the Most Good.*
Isaiah 26:3

ONE DAY WHILE PASSING through the village of Shunem the prophet Elisha was invited by a wealthy couple to share a meal. This soon became a regular thing. Eventually, they added a room for him, where he could rest and pray. It became his home away from home.

Wanting to bless them in return, Elisha asked his assistant, Gehazi, what could be done. Gehazi mentioned the woman was childless and her husband was old. So Elisha called her and said, "About this time next year, you will hold a son in your arms." (2 Kings 4:16)

The woman, overwhelmed, said, "Please, man of God, don't mislead your servant!" The pain of past disappointment made the thought almost unbearable. But a year later, she had a son.

Then one day, when the boy was still a child, he complained of a headache, sat in his mother's lap for a while, and died. Torn with grief, she laid him on Elisha's bed and went to find the prophet.

As she approached Elisha's camp at Mount Carmel, he sent Gehazi to meet her. "Are you all right? Is your husband all right? Is your child all right?"

She replied, "Everything is all right." A strange answer, considering the circumstances.

When she reached Elisha, she fell at his feet. Gehazi tried to move her away, but Elisha said, "Leave her alone! She is in bitter distress, but the Lord has hidden it from me." (2 Kings 4:27)

She said, "Did I ask you for a son? Didn't I tell you, 'Don't raise my hopes'?" (2 Kings 4:28) Then she insisted Elisha come with her.

Elisha went to her home and entered the room where the boy lay. When he saw the child had died, he prayed and stretched himself over him. The boy's body then grew warm. He sneezed seven times and opened his eyes. What a miracle!

Now, let's focus on two details from this story that speak to the topic of God's peace.

First, notice Gehazi's question and the woman's response. He asked if everything was all right with her, her husband, and her son. She said, "Everything is all right." But the Hebrew word used here is significant: *shalom*.

You've likely heard this word before. It's often translated as peace, but it means so much more. It describes harmony, wholeness, completeness, prosperity, and well-being. It describes all that is good. It's more than mere absence of conflict. It's the presence of everything that makes life right.

This woman claimed that everything was "shalom," but it wasn't. Her world had just fallen apart. She said what she needed to say in that moment to get past Gehazi and reach Elisha. But there was no shalom in her soul.

The second detail to note is her earlier response to Elisha's initial promise: "Don't get my hopes up." For her, having a child was everything. She couldn't bear the thought of being disappointed yet again.

Maybe you've prayed something similar. Maybe life has disappointed you more times than you can count, more times that you can bear. You dare not get your hopes up again.

I think we've all been there.

You'll find the promise of peace / shalom all throughout scripture. It's in the gospels: "These things I have spoken unto you that in me you might have peace...Peace I leave with you; my peace I give you...Do not let your hearts be troubled and do not be afraid." (John 16:33; John 14:27)

It's in the Psalms. "The Lord blesses his people with peace." (Psalm 29:11)

And in the letters of St. Paul. "And the peace of God which passes all understanding shall guard your hearts and minds in Christ Jesus." (Philippians 4:7)

It's also found in the writings of Isaiah. One verse in particular not only promises peace, but also provides a simple instruction on how to experience it. And it works, just as it says it will.

Here's the principle, straight and to the point. "You keep him in perfect peace whose mind is stayed on you, because he trusts in you." (Isaiah 26:3 ESV)

This is the promise. When your mind is fixed on God, you experience the kind of peace that the prophet described as "perfect." What does this verse tell us about how to experience perfect peace?

PEACE BEGINS WITH THE THOUGHTS YOU THINK

When life feels chaotic, we often look for an external fix. A drink. A shopping spree. A big bowl of comfort food. We think we need a distraction, but distraction is never the cure. The relief it brings is temporary. Once it fades, the chaos comes back.

Peace begins when, at last, you fully take charge of where your thoughts go and where your thoughts stay. Your mind belongs to you. It's yours to manage. No one else can see what's inside. And no one else can decide what you think about. Only you.

I've learned this on long drives. I'll often make a list of things to think about—plans, projects, favorite memories—because I know that if I don't, my mind will drift. Before I know it, I'm fuming over something someone said 40 years ago or I'm stressed about some situation that doesn't even involve me. That's how peace slips away.

When my grandmother was dying of cancer, my grandfather asked one afternoon if she wanted him to read to her. She said, "No, I'll just lay here and think about good things." She knew she was losing her battle with cancer, but she was determined not to lose the battle of her thoughts. That one was hers to win.

Peace begins in your mind, and it's always something you can do something about.

YOUR THOUGHTS MUST BE CONSISTENTLY FOCUSED

Isaiah says your mind must be *stayed*. Other translations say *steadfast* or *fixed*. The word refers to the ropes and rigging that keep the mast of a ship upright in stormy weather. That's the image he presents. Your thoughts need to be anchored and steady, come what may.

I have a page in my journal where I list all the thoughts I don't allow myself to think. Such as: Don't dwell on what so-and-so said. Don't revisit that memory. Don't tell yourself the situation is hopeless. Don't indulge in self-pity. Don't yield to resentment. I remind myself almost daily: Stay away from these thoughts.

Years ago, Norman Vincent Peale said, "Change your thoughts and you'll change your world." Critics called it simplistic, but anyone who's tried it knows it's not easy. In fact, changing your thoughts is some of the hardest work you'll ever do.

There's a physiological reason for this. With every thought you think, your brain releases a chemical that looks to attach itself to similar thoughts. When you think a thought often enough — positive or negative — your body develops a kind of addiction to it. Your mind begins to crave more of the same.

This is what Marcus Aurelius meant when he said, "The soul becomes dyed with the color of its thoughts." What you dwell on shapes who you are — and whether or not you experience peace.

THE FOCUS OF YOUR THOUGHTS MUST BE ON GOD

Some teach that peace comes from emptying the mind completely. That's not what Scripture teaches. The key is not to clear your mind of all thoughts, but to clear away the clutter so that your thoughts stay centered on Him. God's peace is found in focus.

It's like cleaning your house. You don't throw out the furniture. You just remove what doesn't belong. And you take out the trash. It's the same with your thoughts. Get rid of the mess. Everything not of God needs to go.

Sometimes you'll hear someone say, "I guess I just think too much." No, nobody thinks too much. Everyone thinks the same amount. The question is: What are you thinking about?

If your mind is stayed on God, you'll experience peace. But if it's stayed on regrets, fears, sin, or resentment—peace will forever stay just beyond your reach.

This is why Joshua said, "This Book of the Law shall not depart from your mouth, but you shall meditate in it day and night..." (Joshua 1:8)

It's like the psalmist said, "Oh, how I love your law! It is my meditation all the day." (Psalm 119:97)

And it's why Paul said, "Fix your thoughts on what is true, honorable, right, pure, lovely, and admirable." (Philippians 4:8)

Your thoughts shape your peace. And the more you keep them fixed on God, the more shalom will take root in your life.

CLOSING THOUGHTS

The Shunammite woman experienced a miracle. The promise was fulfilled. Her son was revived. Her heart was renewed. And her shalom was restored.

You and I will witness miracles from time to time. But we're also invited into a greater miracle: the daily fulfillment of God's promises. Especially His promise of peace.

God isn't playing games with you. He's not dangling this promise just out of reach. Shalom is yours when you put yourself in position to receive it.

It begins with a choice. It's where you allow your mind to stay. Every thought leads in one direction or another, toward peace or toward turmoil. When you keep your mind on God, you're demonstrating that you trust in Him. And that's how you open the door to perfect peace.

One thought at a time, shalom becomes reality.

BUILDING MOMENTUM: A LIFE DEFINED BY THE PRESENCE OF GOD'S PEACE.

1 If you were to itemize the thoughts you want to think—the ideas you want filling your mind—what would make your list? And which thoughts would you want to avoid?

2 Have you ever tried to change your thought habits? Was it harder than you expected? What's one area where you've experienced growth leading to victory in your thought life?

3 Consider developing the habit of meditation—intentionally setting your mind on the things of God. What are some specific truths, promises, or attributes of God you could think about?

4 What are some practical ways you can train your mind to "fix" your thoughts throughout the day? Are there routines, reminders, or habits that help you keep your focus on Christ?

_____

_____

_____

_____

_____

5 Can you recall a moment when you experienced deep peace in a stressful time? What was different in that moment, and how did God's presence make itself known to you?

_____

_____

_____

_____

_____

_____

_____

_____

_____

NOTES & IDEAS

THE PROMISE OF PLENTY

This Is What Happens When You Give.
Luke 6:38

A TERM THAT SWEPT the internet not long ago defines an attitude that's long existed in the workforce. You've probably heard it: *Quiet Quitting*.

What is it? According to *The New York Times*: "You're not outright quitting your job, but you're quitting the idea of going above and beyond." In other words, no extra effort without extra pay.

On the same topic, *The Guardian* ran a piece titled, "Why Doing the Bare Minimum Has Gone Global." Around the world, people were taking pride in doing as little as they can.

Actually, this phenomenon isn't new, and it's not limited to the workplace. People have been quiet quitting in every area of life for as long as we've been around.

We often ask: "What's the least I can do and still consider it done? What's the smallest amount expected of me in this job, this position, this relationship, this ministry ... even in my walk with God? What's the bare minimum?"

I remember a bumper sticker from the 1970s: *How much can I sin and still get to heaven?* It was a joke, but many approach the Christian life with a similar mindset: "What are the bottom-rung requirements to get past the pearly gates?"

In this chapter, we'll explore how the quiet quitting mindset—this bare-minimum approach—undermines our giving and robs us of one of the most powerful promises in Scripture.

Jesus said, "Give, and it will be given to you. A good measure, pressed down, shaken together and running over, will be poured into your lap. For with the measure you use, it will be measured to you." (Luke 6:38)

Give, and you'll receive even more than you gave, he's saying. Like every promise in Scripture, you can build your life on these words.

You were made for more than minimums. Every area of your life deserves your best. You have so much to offer, even more than you realize. Jesus is inviting you to join those who are generous, who consistently experience what pressed down, shaken together, and running over is all about.

You can do this even if you don't have two nickels to rub together. This isn't just about money. It's about everything.

GIVING INVOLVES EVERYTHING

Some have the idea that generosity goes no further than their wallets. And they think that wallet-giving is enough.

I've seen people in all kinds of relationships make this mistake. It's easier to write a check or buy a gift than it is to invest time and attention. But generosity involves more than that. Givers give in every area of life.

That's the point Jesus was making when He said, "Do not judge, and you will not be judged. Do not condemn, and you will not be condemned. Forgive, and you will be forgiven." (Luke 6:37)

It's the same principle at work. *What you give is what you get.* When you demonstrate compassion, more compassion comes your way. Forgiveness inspires forgiveness. Mercy makes room for mercy. Scripture says it again and again.

"Those who refresh others will themselves be refreshed." (Proverbs 11:25)

"Blessed are the merciful, for they will be shown mercy." (Matthew 5:7)

"Whoever sows generously will also reap generously." (2 Corinthians 9:6)

You have so much more to give than just what's in your bank account. Your time and attention can often accomplish what money can't. Your service can create value that could surpasses a mere donation. And words of encouragement — there's no price to be put on them.

To be sure, we're called to be generous with our finances. But giving doesn't end there. It reaches into every aspect of life.

GIVING IS A QUALITY AS MUCH AS A QUANTITY

It's not just about the amount. Those who give well understand that the best gifts are given with the right attitude. We need to overcome this mindset of doing the bare minimum and nothing more.

C.S. Lewis suggested that our charitable giving is often done with such condescension toward the recipient and such congratulations toward ourselves that it robs the moment of any real good.

A gift poorly given may meet someone's need, but it can also be used to knock them down a peg. You've seen it happen, no doubt. Let's not be guilty of this. We can give in a way that not only meets a person's need, it builds them up as well.

I knew a business owner who would include handwritten notes in his employees' envelopes each payday. He'd write things like, "Thanks for doing a great job. Thanks for going the extra mile. Thanks for helping this business succeed."

He couldn't afford big bonuses, but he made sure his people felt appreciated.

He said he learned it from one of his own employees. Years earlier, a woman on his team would often say when she received her check, "By the way, thanks for this job. And thanks for being such a great boss." Her attitude changed his. He had always believed that a paycheck was all that mattered. But her gratitude made him want to do more.

Giving is a *quality*. That's why Scripture says, "God loves a cheerful giver." (2 Corinthians 9:7)

Have you ever received a gift that was beautifully wrapped, with thoughtful detail? Even though the paper ends up in the trash, the care taken in the presentation makes the gift feel more special.

Compare that with the last-minute gift stuffed in a plastic bag, price tag still attached.

That's the difference quality makes.

Father Medard Laz once wrote, "Obligation can pour a glass of milk, but quite often love adds a little chocolate." Good-measure giving recognizes that how you give matters. Even if you can't give as much as you'd like, you can always give in the best way you can.

GIVING IS A LONG DISTANCE RUN

One reason Amazon became so successful is that, from the beginning, the leadership team thought long-term. While most companies focused on quarterly profits and immediate returns, they were planning for decades down the road.

This concept isn't new. A *New York Times* article from the 1980s made the same comparison between American and Japanese companies: American firms expected instant results; Japanese companies took the long view.

The same principle applies to our giving. We don't give today just so God will bless us tomorrow. That's not how it works. Giving is about long-term obedience.

Sometimes there's a gap between when you give and when you receive. You may feel like you're doing all you can do in your relationships, your work, even your pursuit of holiness, but you're still not getting results.

If giving were a sprint, maybe you'd have a reason to quit. But it's not. It's a marathon. A long-distance run. This is why Paul reminds us, "Let us not become weary in doing good, for at the proper time we will reap a harvest if we do not give up." (Galatians 6:9)

In *Tortured for Christ*, Lutheran pastor Richard Wurmbrand tells how he spent years in and out of Communist prisons for preaching the gospel. He was tortured, starved, and isolated.

And yet, he never lost the habit of tithing.

He was given one bowl of dirty soup each day and one slice of stale bread per week. Every tenth day he gave his soup, and every tenth week his bread, to someone weaker than himself.

Why would he do this?

Because he understood the promises of God. He knew that giving isn't about instant results. It's about faithfulness over the course of time.

The Christian life isn't just a little jaunt. It's a long haul. It's a journey from one world to the next. And it's a race worth running well.

When you live as a good-measure giver, the blessings will find their way to you. Not always today, not always tomorrow, but at the proper time.

So get ready to go the distance.

CLOSING THOUGHTS

Quiet quitting isn't just about laziness. At its core, it's about selfishness. It's the me-first mindset: I want what I want, I want it now, and I'll do the least I can to get it.

But that's no way to live. There's a better path to take. It leads to joy, purpose, and fulfillment. Instead of giving the very least, choose to give your very best in every area of life. And trust God with the results in His perfect timing.

It's been said there are two kinds of people in the world: Givers and takers. And while the takers may eat better, but the givers sleep better.

I'll add something to that statement.

Givers *live better* in every way that matters: Pressed down. Shaken together. Running over.

BUILDING MOMENTUM: EXPERIENCE THE BLESSING OF GENEROSITY

1 Are there areas of your life where you're tempted to give less than your best? What holds you back from giving fully?

2 Setting aside the subject of money, what are some other ways and other areas where you can increase your giving?

3 In your daily tasks and obligations, is there a way to "add a little chocolate" to the service you provide for others?

4 Can you think of a time when you gave generously and didn't see immediate results, or didn't receive anything in return? How did you respond? Are you willing to plant seeds of generosity and trust God with the timing of the harvest?

NOTES & IDEAS

NOTES & IDEAS

THE PROMISE OF GOD'S CANCEL-FREE COVENANT

Our Lives Can Be Built on This Irrevocable Word.
Hebrews 8:8-12

A FRIEND TOLD ME recently that during a family event, someone brought up a mistake he'd made when he was barely out of high school—more than thirty years ago. It didn't take long for a couple of others to join in.

"It was like facing cancel culture without the internet," he said. "I just wanted to leave."

He was surprised—and deeply moved—when his daughter stepped in, setting the others straight: "I don't think anyone here is in a position to throw stones. Let's move on." Good for her.

We see this tendency to never forget and not quite forgive everywhere: in marriages, families, friendships, communities, businesses, and churches. The unspoken verdict is that your past defines you, and it always will.

That's the way of the world. But Scripture's great promise stands in radical opposition. While the crowd says, "We'll never let go of what you did," the Holy God of Israel says, "I will forgive you and remember your sins no more."

The writer of Hebrews quotes the prophet Jeremiah:

"The days are coming," declares the Lord, "when I will make a new covenant...It will not be like the covenant I made with their ancestors...I will put my laws in their minds and write them on their hearts. I will be their God, and they will be my people...For I will forgive their wickedness and will remember their sins no more." (Hebrews 8:8–12)

God is making a promise that sounds almost too good to be true: You can be forgiven—once and for all and forever. The sins of your past, no matter the number, will be remembered no more.

This is the New Covenant we experience in Jesus Christ.

The word *covenant* typically refers to a contract—a mutual agreement between equals. But in Hebrews, the Greek word used here refers not to a contract, but to a will.

That's a huge difference.

Contracts are negotiated between parties. In a will, the terms are established by the giver. Contracts require reciprocal effort, where each party does their part. In a will, nothing is reciprocal. One gives and the other receives.

This is how God relates to His people. He doesn't say, "Do your part, and I'll do mine." He says, "I've done all there is to do. It's yours for the asking."

That's good news, especially when you realize that sometimes it's not the world holding you back—it's you. Many of us are inclined to cancel ourselves, to look at past sins and say, "I don't believe God could forgive me for this." Scripture makes it clear that He has chosen not to distance Himself from you. He has chosen, instead, to draw you into His presence, to wash away your sin, and to make you holy—once and for all and forever.

You may be familiar with the Old Covenant. You may have even tried living by it, thinking you could earn God's favor.

If you tried, you failed.

The writer of Hebrews tells us the Old Covenant is no longer in effect. There is a New Covenant available to everyone everywhere—to all who are ready to receive it.

AS MANY SECOND CHANCES AS IT TAKES

"I will make a new covenant... It will not be like the one I made with their ancestors... They did not remain faithful... But this is the new covenant I will make." (Hebrews 8:8–10)

Though His people failed to keep the Old Covenant, God promised an even better one—one that all could keep. That's because our God is the God of the second chance. And the third chance. And the fourth. And the four-hundredth and the five-thousandth.

Is it really true? Do we get that many chances?

Yes. Because we *need* that many chances.

Throughout the Old Testament, God's people walked away from Him again and again. And again and again, when they returned, He restored them. That's because He's the God of mercy. The God of forgiveness. The God of another chance.

Whenever we talk about God's relentless mercy, someone always asks: "Does this mean I can sin all I want, and God will just keep forgiving me?"

It's not that you sin all you want. The truth is you'll sin more than you want. Way more. When you surrender your life to Jesus Christ, you become a new creation. The Holy Spirit begins conforming you to the image of God's Son, and you develop the desire to distance yourself from the old life.

But it doesn't happen overnight.

I don't know how long the process takes. I only know that it takes more than 48 years. (That's how long I've been at it.) You'll discover that you stumble more than you'd like. And you'll learn that falling on your face never brings the same satisfaction as walking in step with Christ.

Sometimes that realization leads to frustration, even despair. That's when you need to remember the foundation of the New Covenant. It's built on second chances.

If your image of God is a stern figure with folded arms and a disapproving glare, you're not seeing Him through the lens of the New Covenant. You're not hearing Him say, "I won't give up on those who call My name. Even though they've failed before, I'll give them another chance."

This isn't about taking God's mercy for granted. It's about living in the confidence of His love. When you fall, He wants you to try again. When you wander, He wants you to come back.

IT'S ALL ABOUT A PERSONAL RELATIONSHIP WITH GOD

"I will put my laws in their minds and write them on their hearts. I will be their God, and they will be my people." (Hebrews 8:10)

Years ago, I worked for a man who had been a close friend for quite some time. My job was to help coordinate a publishing project with a team of colleagues and outside contributors.

Throughout the process, when decisions had to be made, I could often say, "John will want it done this way." And I was usually right.

How did I know? Because he was my friend. I knew his values. I knew how he thought. I didn't need an employee handbook to make the right call, because I knew him.

That's what God is saying here.

He has no interest in a distant, rulebook-only relationship. Instead, He says, "I will write my laws on their hearts." In other words, "I will be known by them. Personally."

This means your relationship is not with a book. Or a building. Or a denomination. Or a preacher. It's with Him, personally.

Yes, we benefit greatly from the Bible and the local church. But your life is in Him, and Him alone. Hebrews 8:11 says, "And they will not need to teach their neighbors, nor will they need to teach their relatives, saying, 'You should know the Lord.' For everyone, from the least to the greatest, will know Me already."

He's not saying we don't need teachers or preachers. He's saying we don't need mediators. You don't need a go-between. No one on earth—absolutely no one—has more access to God than you do. In this relationship, we're all equal. *Everyone, from the least to the greatest, will know Me already.*

That's the beauty of the New Covenant. Your connection to God doesn't depend on your church membership, or your pastor's approval, or how many verses you've memorized.

The church plays an essential role in helping you grow. It offers accountability. It provides opportunities to serve. But it can never take the place of your relationship with God. Nor can any preacher or any church position themselves between you and Jesus.

God has made Himself available to you. Personally.

He says, "You will know Me."

EVERY DAY IS A NEW BEGINNING

"And I will forgive their wickedness, and I will never again remember their sins." (Hebrews 8:12)

Some see it as their calling to highlight your every misstep, time and again. On social media, even complete strangers volunteer for the task. No doubt you've noticed.

While the world keeps a permanent record of your past, God promises to do something completely different: He forgives and He forgets.

"He has removed our sins as far from us as the east is from the west." (Psalm 103:12)

"You have put all my sins behind Your back." (Isaiah 38:17)

"You trample our sins under Your feet and throw them into the depths of the ocean." (Micah 7:19)

When God forgives, He erases the record. He doesn't revisit your worst moments or replay your biggest failures. He chooses not to remember them at all.

The prophet Jeremiah said, "His mercies never come to an end; they are new every morning." (Lamentations 3:22-23) Each day is a fresh start, a new beginning.

This means you don't have to live under yesterday's shame. You don't have to carry around the weight of what you did, who you hurt, or who you used to be. God says, "And I will forgive their wickedness, and I will never again remember their sins." (Hebrews 8:12)

And He says, "If we confess our sins to Him, He is faithful and just to forgive us our sins and to cleanse us from all wickedness." (1 John 1:9 NASB)

He's not holding your sins over your head. He's not keeping score. The New Covenant is a clean slate. That means no more guilt. No more shame. No more condemnation.

Just forgiveness. And another chance.

CLOSING THOUGHTS

The world will hold on to your past and use it against you.

But God lets it go. He casts it aside to make room for a new life—a fresh start—as He conforms you to the image of His Son, Jesus Christ.

As long as we live in this broken world, there will be those who refuse to let go of your past, who refuse to let you move on.

But the One who matters most—the Holy God of Israel—has declared: "I will forgive their wickedness, and I will remember their sins no more." (Hebrews 8:12)

You belong to God. You are forgiven once and for all and forever. Your past is gone. Your future is secure.

You can build your life on this beautiful promise, God's "no more" really means no more.

BUILDING MOMENTUM: A LIFE FUELED BY SECOND CHANCES.

1 Have you ever needed a second chance? Has someone else ever needed a second chance from you? How did it feel to offer (or receive) such grace? Were you reluctant, or did it come easily?

---

2 What role does the church play in your relationship with God? Is it possible to grow spiritually without being part of a community of faith, or is something missing?

---

3 In what ways does Scripture shape your connection to God? Could someone have a strong relationship with Him apart from the Bible? Why or why not?

---

4 Is there a difference between *forgetting someone's sin* and *choosing not to remember*? What does that difference look like? What does it mean to practice Biblical forgiveness in real life?

5 Do you ever find yourself keeping track of the failures and offenses of others? What helps you let go of that record and show mercy instead?

NOTES & IDEAS

NOTES & IDEAS

The Next Step

The promises of God were never meant to remain on the page. They're meant to be lived. Day by day, moment by moment, you can use them to define the direction of your life and shape its very outcome.

So, now we've reached the part where you take the next step.

This step may be as simple as setting aside time each day to meet with God in prayer, and to study His Word. That's certainly a good place to begin.

It could also mean committing to serve more faithfully, to give more generously, to pray more boldly.

Or maybe this step is about calling on the courage to try once again to live the life you know that God has designed for you. Where you're no longer discouraged by the past. Where you're now empowered by all He has spoken.

Here's where every promise-filled journey begins. It's one intentional step of faith followed by another. Each is yours to take. This is how you build your life on God's everlasting goodness.

What will your next step be?

About the Author

STEVE MAY has spent more than thirty years serving the church as a pastor, missionary, worship leader, and teacher. Throughout his ministry, his focus has been to help people discover a faith grounded in Scripture and made visible in daily life.

Steve is the author of twelve books. He also serves as editor of Preaching Library, providing practical study and research resources for those who preach and teach God's Word.

Steve's Monday Memo devotional is read each week by thousands of pastors and ministry leaders.

You can find out more about Steve at **stevemay.com**.

Also by Steve May

IT'S ALL IN THE DAILIES
Setting the Scene for an Epic Life

THE EVENTS OF YOUR LIFE may not seem all that impressive when viewed a few frames at a time. However, it is the discipline you establish and the good habits you practice frame-by-frame that can make your life an Oscar-winning epic.

This book, consisting of more than 100 daily devotionals, is designed to help you make the most of each day, giving this life your best performance every morning, noon, and night.

"If any of you wants to be my follower, you must first turn from your selfish ways, take up your cross *daily*, and follow me." (Luke 9:23)

It's all in the dailies.

Available in print and Kindle format.

Also by Steve May

NEVER LOSE HEART
Life Lifting Lessons from 2 Corinthians 4:16-18

THE LESSONS in this brief study explain why it's always too soon to quit ... but it's never too late to start. It's too soon to quit, or even think about quitting, because God will fulfill his promise in our lives. And it's never too late to fully invest in God's plan for your future.

Taken from 2 Corinthians 4:16-18, the principles taught in these few verses can help us all remain steady in our resolve to *Never Lose Heart*.

Ideal for group or individual study. Each chapter includes follow-up questions and suggestions for reflection and group discussion.

Available in print and Kindle format.

VISIT STEVEMAY.COM

www.ingramcontent.com/pod-product-compliance
Lightning Source LLC
Chambersburg PA
CBHW060336050426
42449CB00011B/2770